Ding Dong Bell

OXFORD

Ding dong bell,
Pussy's in the well.

Who put her in?
Little Tommy Thin.

Who pulled her out?
Little Johnny Stout.

What a naughty boy was that
to try to drown poor pussy cat,

who never did him any harm,

and caught the mice in his
father's barn.

Oxford University Press, Great Clarendon Street, Oxford, OX2 6DP

Oxford New York
Athens Auckland Bangkok Bogota Buenos Aires
Calcutta Cape Town Chennai Dar es Salaam Delhi
Florence Hong Kong Istanbul Karachi Kuala Lumpur
Madrid Melbourne Mexico City Mumbai Nairobi
Paris São Paulo Singapore Taipei Tokyo
Toronto Warsaw

and associated companies in
Berlin Ibadan

Oxford is a trade mark of Oxford University Press

The Phonics Starter Pack contains:
Big Nursery Rhyme Book ISBN 0 19 915596 8
Nursery Rhyme Books (six titles) ISBN 0 19 915588 7
Big ABC Book ISBN 0 19 915597 6
Sound Books (30 titles) ISBN 0 19 915598 4
Sound Activity Cards ISBN 0 19 915599 2
Phonics Teacher's Guide ISBN 0 19 915600 X

Printed in Hong Kong
Series Editor: Clare Kirtley

ISBN 0 19 9155836

Published by Oxford University Press 1999